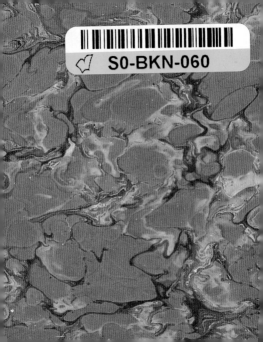

Fathers

Fathers

Edited by Bridget Sullivan

Ariel Books

ANDREWS AND McMEEL

KANSAS CITY

ISBN : 0-8362-1054-9

Library of Congress Catalog Card Number : 95-80741

Fathers

*I*ntroduction

Stern patriarchs or secret pussycats, ungrouchy Grouchos or very cool Coolidges, fathers are here aplenty. They love, they cherish, they instruct, they dispense wisdom and foolishness, and—if we are fortunate—they are always there for us. In these pages you will find stories about the great, the brilliant, the rich, the famous, the ordinary, and the extraordinary—those who taught us so much of what we know— our dads. To fathers everywhere, and to the sons and daughters who fulfill their lives, we dedicate this little book.

Of course there were areas of safety; nothing could get at me if I curled up on my father's lap, holding on to his ear with one thumb tucked into it. . . . All about him was safe.

NAOMI MITCHISON

After JFK was assassinated, his young son, John, asked William Haddad, an associate of Kennedy's, "Are you a daddy?" Haddad admitted that he was. Said little John, "Then will you throw me up in the air?"

When Charles first saw our child Mary, he said all the proper things for a new father. He looked upon the poor little red thing and blurted, "She's more beautiful than the Brooklyn Bridge."

HELEN HAYES

*N*ever raise your
hand to your
children; it leaves
your midsection
unprotected.

ROBERT ORBEN

13

Now that I have two daughters, I realize if a fellow like me came around and dated my girls, I don't think I would let him in the front door.

GEORGE ARCHER

I remember being at a point below his knees and looking up at the vast length of him. He was six foot three; his voice was big. He was devastatingly attractive—even to his daughter as a child. . . . His voice was so beautiful, so enveloping. He was just bigger and better than anyone else.

ANJELICA HUSTON

*W*hat matters to me is not how I look, but the person inside, the one who grew up as—and is forever proud to be—the daughter of Bill Shepherd.

CYBILL SHEPHERD

When I was a boy of fourteen, my father was so ignorant I could hardly stand to have the old man around. But when I got to be twenty-one, I was astonished at how much he had learned in seven years.

MARK TWAIN

My father was a conservative Republican. When the New Yorker published a profile of Franklin Delano Roosevelt, he canceled our subscription.

JULIA CHILD

The father is always a Republican toward his son, and his mother's always a Democrat.

ROBERT FROST

It is impossible to please all the world and also one's father.

JEAN DE LA FONTAINE

 19

There have been many times when I thought other people might be better singers or better musicians or prettier than me, but then I would hear Daddy's voice telling me to never say never, and I would find a way to squeeze an extra inch or two out of what God had given me.

BARBARA MANDRELL

*M*y father hated radio and could not wait for television to be invented so he could hate that too.

PETER DE VRIES

I guess the only thing that's important is that he was *my father*. He was some guy, my dad was. Some guy.

JACK LEMMON

I teach my child to look at life in a thoroughly materialistic fashion. If he escapes and becomes the sort of person I hope he will become, it will be because he sees through the hokum that I hand out.

E. B. WHITE

My father always told me that you have to be true to yourself before you can give your best to others— professionally and personally.

NANCY WILSON

I was always terrified of what my father was going to say to the press. When they asked him what he thought of the permissive society he said he wished to God it had been invented sixty years ago!

EDWARD HEATH

*O*ne of these days in your travels, a guy is going to come up to you and show you a nice, brand-new deck of cards on which the seal is not yet broken, and this guy is going to offer to bet you that he can make the jack of spades jump out of the deck and squirt cider in your ear. But, son, do not bet this man, for as sure as you stand there, you are going to wind up with an earful of cider.

DAMON RUNYON
(ADVICE FROM HIS FATHER)

*O*ld as she was, she still missed
her daddy sometimes.

GLORIA NAYLOR

*M*y father always wanted to be
the corpse at every funeral, the bride
at every wedding, and the baby
at every christening.

ALICE ROOSEVELT LONGWORTH
(OF HER FATHER,
THEODORE ROOSEVELT)

Fathers are something else. They always give up their turn by saying something like, "Go ask your mother. She knows about things like that."

MARY KUCZKIR

I didn't know the full facts of life until I was seventeen. My father never talked about his work.

MARTIN FREUD

This is what a father ought to be about: helping his son to form the habit of doing right on his own initiative, rather than because he's afraid of some serious consequence.

TERENCE

Never have partners.

HOWARD HUGHES'S FATHER

This is a moment that I deeply wish my parents could have lived to share. My father would have enjoyed what you have so generously said of me — and my mother would have believed it.

LYNDON B. JOHNSON

*My father was an intellectual
and our home was filled with talk.*

*The most important thing a father
can do for his children is to love
their mother.*

I've wondered, over the years, as I've recalled these moments with my father, what they're supposed to teach me about life. I can't say there's any lesson, except the sheer pleasure of his company, which was a great gift, and which I gather is sometimes hard to come by between fathers and sons.

SCOTT SIMON

My mother said he [my father] was proud of me and I suppose he was. But he was very Germanic and didn't like to show emotions. The first decent season I had I conducted the Philharmonic in New York and at Cleveland, Philadelphia, and Minneapolis. When I told him, all he said was, "So they didn't want you at Boston, then?"

ANDRÉ PREVIN

 33

Fathers, provoke not your children to anger, lest they be discouraged.

COLOSSIANS 3:21

*W*e think our fathers fools,

so wise we grow;

Our wiser sons, no doubt

will think us so.

ALEXANDER POPE

*T*o bring up a child in the way

he should go, travel that way

yourself once in a while.

JOSH BILLINGS

(HENRY WHEELER SHAW)

My father was an M.D. and a surgeon, and he used to take me on house calls. I grew up in a farm community, and many of these trips were way out in the country, so we had lots of time in the car. That's where we really talked to each other.

BOB MATHIAS

What greater ornament to a son
than a father's glory, or to a father
than a son's honorable conduct?

SOPHOCLES

I've always had the feeling I could
do anything; my daddy told me I
could, and I was in college before I
found out he might be wrong.

ANN RICHARDS

38

When I was made presidential press secretary my father sent me a telegram: "Always tell the truth. If you can't always tell the truth, don't lie."

BILL MOYERS

Where does the family start?
It starts with a young man
in love with a girl—
no superior alternative
has yet been found.

WINSTON CHURCHILL

I watched a small man with thick calluses on both hands work fifteen and sixteen hours a day. I saw him once literally bleed from the bottoms of his feet, a man who came here uneducated, alone, unable to speak the language, who taught me all I needed to know about faith and hard work by the simple eloquence of his example.

MARIO CUOMO

The fundamental defect of fathers

is that they want their children

to be a credit to them.

BERTRAND RUSSELL

A wise son maketh a

glad father . . .

PROVERBS 10:1

*O*f course my father was a great influence on me. He taught me how to read.

MICHAEL FOOT

*M*y father was the dominant person in our family and in my life.

JIMMY CARTER

 43

*One father is more than
a hundred schoolmasters.*

ENGLISH PROVERB

*He was a special person
and I loved him very much.
He was my dad.*

NELLIE PIKE RANDALL

44

My father . . . used to bounce me on his knee when I was five years old and say, "Movies, movies, movies." So obviously something sank in.

NATASHA RICHARDSON
(OF HER FATHER,
TONY RICHARDSON)

Deep in the cavern of the
infant's breast
The father's nature lurks,
and lives anew.

HORACE

The sooner you treat your son as a
man, the sooner he will be one.

JOHN DRYDEN

*You're a kind of father
figure to me, Dad.*

ALAN COREN

*What a father says to his
children is not heard by the world,
but it will be heard by posterity.*

JEAN PAUL RICHTER

*A*ll men know
their children
mean more than life.
If childless people sneer—
Well, they've less
sorrow. But what
lonesome luck!

EURIPIDES

. . . We know that men can rear children, in a slightly different way from mothers but—so far as we can tell—no less effectively.

JOHN NICHOLSON

An angry father is most cruel toward himself.

PUBLILIUS SYRUS

*I*t is no new observation, I believe, that a lover in most cases has no rival so much to be feared as the father.

CHARLES LAMB

I talk and talk and talk, and I haven't taught people in fifty years what my father taught by example in one week.

MARIO CUOMO

 51

The first big-league game I ever saw was at the Polo Grounds. My father took me. I remember it so well—the green grass and the green stands. It was like seeing Oz.

JOHN CURTIS

Never get sick, Hubert, there isn't time.

HUBERT HUMPHREY'S FATHER

I was fourteen when my father died. I miss everything about him. He taught us that we shouldn't be people of success, we should be people of values, because that was the only thing that endured.

ROBERT F. KENNEDY JR.

You don't raise heroes, you raise sons. And if you treat them like sons, they'll turn out to be heroes, even if it's just in your own eyes.

To become a father is not hard, To be a father is, however.

WILHELM BUSCH

*Happy that man whose children
make his happiness in life
and not his grief.*

EURIPIDES

*My father was not a failure.
After all, he was the father of a
president of the United States.*

HARRY S. TRUMAN

My father was two men, one sympathetic and intuitional, the other critical and logical; altogether they formed a combination that could not be thrown off its feet.

JULIAN HAWTHORNE
(OF HIS FATHER,
NATHANIEL HAWTHORNE)

*A*nything which a father has not learned from experience he can now learn from his children.

ANONYMOUS

*W*ith him for a sire and her for a dam,
What should I be but just what I am?

EDNA ST. VINCENT MILLAY

 57

The first-time father, beside himself with excitement over the birth of his son, was determined to follow all the rules to a T. "So tell me, Nurse," he asked as his new family headed out the hospital door, "what time should we wake the little guy in the morning?"

ANONYMOUS

My best training came
from my father.

WOODROW WILSON

*W*hat law is it that says a woman is a better parent simply because of her sex? I guess I've had to think a lot about whatever it is that makes somebody a good parent: constancy, patience, understanding . . . love. Where is it written that a man has any less of those qualities than a woman?

TED, IN *KRAMER VS. KRAMER*

It's clear that most American children suffer too much mother and too little father.

GLORIA STEINEM

I remember once when I was very young and I was looking at his navel and asked him what that was. And he said, "That's where Custer shot me." Because I knew who Custer was. And I believed that for years—until the point I realized that I had one too, and I didn't get shot.

WILLIAM LEAST HEAT MOON

Build me a son, O Lord, who will be strong enough to know when he is weak, and brave enough to face himself when he is afraid, one who will be proud and unbending in honest defeat, and humble and gentle in victory.

DOUGLAS MACARTHUR
(*A FATHER'S PRAYER*)

$\mathcal{H}$e who raises the child is called
the father, not the one who had
begotten the child.

MIDRASH RABBAH

*B*ack in 1880 when I was a child, I asked my father for a cent. He heard me gravely and then informed me just as gravely that it looked to him as if a Democratic president would be elected that fall, and it behooved every prudent man to exercise especial thrift. Therefore, he would be obliged to deny my request.

CALVIN COOLIDGE

It's only when you grow up, and step back from him, or leave him for your own career and your own home — it's only then that you can measure his greatness and fully appreciate it. Pride reinforces love.

MARGARET TRUMAN

Any father whose son raises his hand against him is guilty: of having produced a son who raised his hand against him.

CHARLES PÉGUY

A daughter is to her father a treasure of sleeplessness.

APOCRYPHA

68

The kind of man who thinks that helping with the dishes is beneath him will also think that helping with the baby is beneath him, and then he certainly is not going to be a very successful father.

ELEANOR ROOSEVELT

I have found the best way to give advice to your children is to find out what they want and then advise them to do it.

HARRY S. TRUMAN

Parents are not quite interested in justice, they are interested in quiet.

BILL COSBY

A man finds out what is meant by a spitting image when he tries to feed cereal to his infant.

IMOGENE FEY

*I*t is a wise father that knows his own child.

WILLIAM SHAKESPEARE

Every parent is at some time the father of the unreturned prodigal, with nothing to do but keep his house open to hope.

JOHN CIARDI

I lived with my father only six years, the first six years of my life, but I remember vividly so many of his characteristics, and I still find myself emulating them. My mother taught me my ABCs. From my father I learned the glories of going to the bathroom outside.

LEWIS GRIZZARD

Every day of my life has been a gift from him. His lap had been my refuge from lightning and thunder. His arms had sheltered me from teen-age heartbreak. His wisdom and understanding had sustained me as an adult.

NELLIE PIKE RANDALL

You don't have to deserve your mother's love. You have to deserve your father's. He's more particular.

ROBERT FROST

Be perfectly natural with people of high rank, but with everyone else please behave like an Englishman.

WOLFGANG AMADEUS MOZART'S FATHER

He was strong rather than profound . . . I often wonder about him. In my struggle to be a writer, it was he who supported and backed me and explained me—not my mother.

JOHN STEINBECK

*T*he time not to become a father is
eighteen years before a world war.

E. B. WHITE

The little Dad owned he took care of. He had a farmer's respect for tools. He kept his pocketknife sharp. He edged it on an oilstone, careful of the angle. . . . He polished his own shoes and taught us to polish ours. One of his belts was carefully stitched together in back where it had broken. Good shoes and belts, he'd tell us, would last fifteen years.

RICHARD RHODES

This book

was set in

Cochin and

Isadora

•

Book design

by

Barbara M.

Bachman

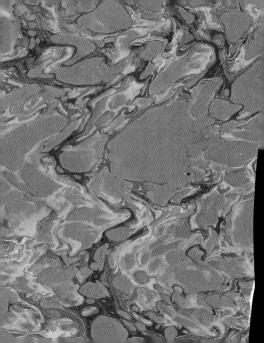